THE MENTOR I NEVER MET

LESSONS ON LIFE AND BUSINESS FROM JOHN CAPOBIANCO

PAUL J. SCOTT

Copyright © 2022 by Paul J. Scott

All rights reserved.

No part of this publication may be reproduced, stored in a retrieval system, or transmitted in any form or by any means, electronic, mechanical, photocopying, recording or otherwise without the prior permission of the publisher or in accordance with the provisions of the Copyright, Designs and Patents Act of 1988 or under the terms of any license permitting limited copying issued by the Copyright Licensing Agency.

Published by:

Paul J. Scott | Boston, Massachusetts

Cover Design:

GoingClear | Branding, Marketing & Digital Agency

CONTENTS

Introduction	vii
1. A Great Man From Humble Beginnings	1
2. You Make Your Own Luck	5
3. The Next Opportunity	11
4. A Growing Business	16
5. Italia Rose	22
6. A Family Man	29
7. Dinnertime	33
8. Becoming a Legend	41
9. The Fullness of Life	48
10. My Great-Grandfather's Legacy	60
Thank You, John	65
Appendix: Capobianco Construction Photos	68
Notes	81

This book is dedicated to my mother, Marguerite, who passed away while I was writing about her grandfather and his influence on my life.

I love you, Mum, thank you for everything you did for me. I'll never forget.

Also, a very special thank you to my Aunt Judy for all the stories, and for answering my countless questions about my great grandfather.

INTRODUCTION

One of my heroes is a man I've never met.

That isn't so unusual. Growing up, you might have idolized a sports star, an astronaut, or even a superhero. Maybe you liked reading about actors or scientists. Whoever it was, you probably didn't know any of these people personally. In some cases, they may not have even existed. I certainly had those kinds of role models, too. But the one who cast the biggest shadow over my life was a relative who passed several years before I was born. He was my great-grandfather, John Capobianco. Some knew him as Giovanni Capobianco, but he was "Papa" to his family who knew him best.

My whole life I heard stories about him from my mother, my aunts, my grandfather Alphonse, and even my extended family. I was always especially fascinated by the stories that came from my mom. I always wanted to learn more and more. From a young age I learned how he represented so many different parts of the American ideal. My great-grandfather John was an immigrant who arrived virtually penniless from Italy. He went on to become a successful entrepreneur and was known throughout his community as being a generous family man. In short, my great-grandfather was everything I wanted to grow up to be.

Although most people outgrow their attachment to their childhood heroes, I never lost my fascination with Great-Grandfather John. As I made my way through life, and eventually became an entrepreneur myself, a part of me felt as if I were following in his footsteps.

Over the last few years, however, I realized there were gaps in my knowledge about the man whose stories were still impacting me more than a century later. Everything I had heard convinced me that he had the sort of life we might all be trying to emulate, but there were parts I didn't know. Eventually, my curiosity drove me to find the photos, genealogical records, and (most importantly) stories he left behind. This short book is the result of my search.

What started as a way to record what I learned about my great-grandfather, and our family history, turned into something bigger. It's the tale of one man's life and determination. It's also something I hope my relatives can hold on to for generations to come. But most of all it's a reminder of what you can achieve when your heart and mind are in the right place.

I wish I had gotten the chance to know my great-grandfather John personally. Since I didn't, these pages have to serve as my thank-you to him – both for the example he set and for all he has done for my family.

Most of the people reading these pages probably won't have met my great-grandfather, either. I hope you will follow along anyway. Not only is his story one of love, adventure, and inspiration, but I think he would like the idea of sharing what he had learned with a wider audience. Everyone I've talked to who *does* remember Great-Grandfather John has a story about his generous spirit. He did a lot of things the hard way so that his kids, grandkids, and neighbors didn't have to.

So, if you're interested in the tale of an immigrant who arrived with nothing and eventually got all he dreamed of (and more), let's start at the very beginning of his journey...

1

A GREAT MAN FROM HUMBLE BEGINNINGS

My great-grandfather didn't start life as "Great-Grandfather John," of course. In fact, like many of history's most prominent and ambitious people, he came from inauspicious beginnings.

Born in the small southern Italian town of Sturno, near Napoli, John entered the world on August 29, 1888. There isn't a great deal we know about his early life and family, except to say that his parents, Giuseppe and Marguerite, were very religious people. Not only did they walk to mass regularly – a habit my great-grandfather continued throughout his life – but his brother devoted his life to the Catholic faith, eventually becoming a cardinal.

Even today, Sturno is known as a small farming community where sheep and goats are as common as the people who look after them. Back in John's day it would have been the sort of place where families knew their neighbors and said hello when they passed in the streets. He would tell his daughters and grandchildren stories about walking through the town square on Sundays, or during festivals, with everyone dressed in their single set of clothes that was reserved for special occasions.

As fondly as he remembered these times, though, it would have been tough to imagine a future near his birthplace. Most of Italy was struggling financially in the late nineteenth century, and the Avellino province where Sturno sits was hit particularly hard by recession. It's not hard to picture a setting where farmers, priests, and shopkeepers could eke out a living, but a young person might have to look elsewhere if they wanted to make a name for themselves.

It isn't known whether my great-grandfather had big ambitions or if his parents just wanted him to enjoy a more prosperous life than they did. It could even be that they struggled to feed the growing boy in their home. Whatever the specific reason, at the turn of the century they made the decision to put John on a boat that was headed for New York. He was just 12 years old at the time.

If the thought of sending a boy, not even yet a teenager, on a long journey to a continent you have never visited seems painful, just imagine what it would have been like for him. Although those sorts of adventurous travels were *relatively* more common for children then, it didn't mean they were going to be easy.

Back in those days America was very literally still "the New World" to much of Europe. It doesn't appear as if my great-grandfather had any relatives to join up with. Nor did he have contacts or even a plan beyond "find a better life than we can give you in Italy." That's not a lot to go on.

Even if there were more preparation, the trip would still have been dangerous. Today, you can take a nonstop flight that will send you from Rome to New York (or vice versa) in around nine hours. In those days making the trip meant weeks on a boat. Storms, diseases, and common criminals were all accepted risks. It wouldn't have been that uncommon for someone to perish, or just disappear, along the way.

Poor as they might have been, my great-grandfather's family didn't ship him off from his home empty-handed. As a gift to help him launch his new life, they provided him with the tidy sum of $200. That works out to just over $5,500 at the time of this writing if you adjust for inflation. It wasn't much, but they would have presumably scrimped, saved, and sold whatever they could to send him with *something* he could use to get established once he arrived.

Naturally, they were wary of sending a young boy to a new country with all of that cash. So, they found an acquaintance who would be making the same voyage and asked him to safeguard both the funds and the child. He agreed, and did his part to ensure John arrived at Ellis Island with the other passengers. When the time came to exchange the money, however, he disappeared. Neither my great-grandfather, nor his family, ever heard from the man again.

With that, John found himself young, lost, and penniless in one of the world's fastest-growing cities. He had no contacts, little education, and a very slight grasp on the English language. He must have known that the years ahead weren't going to be easy. That was all right; he always was one to rise to a challenge.

Vintage photo of Ellis Island as I imagine John might have seen it as he approached New York.

2

YOU MAKE YOUR OWN LUCK

They say art imitates life, but sometimes the real world gives you situations that would be too unbelievable for a Hollywood script. Imagine my great-grandfather, in New York City at the turn of the 20th century, trying to find the next step with no money or connections. The "better life" his parents had in mind for him probably didn't involve someone stealing all of his savings and leaving him to fend for himself.

I don't know how he managed to survive those first few days and weeks, and to the best of my knowledge he didn't talk about it later in life. He might have begged strangers for money. Or, having come from a devout family, he could have visited a church and asked for bread or mercy. My instincts tell me he probably didn't do either of those things. Instead, he likely did what he was known for later in life and *just got to work*.

New York was a growing city in 1900, filled with immigrants from all over Europe. It wouldn't have been unusual for a boy, even one as young as he was, to get a job. My guess is that he found someone who would accept his hard labor for a place to sleep and the occasional warm meal. He probably did odd jobs for pennies. It would have been grueling work, but I doubt that would have deterred him. He had come to America for a fresh start and you could be sure he was going to get one.

I'm speculating a little bit, but there *are* two things I know about this period in John's life. The first is that he eventually matured enough physically to find work as a bricklayer. That would have been a notoriously difficult and taxing job. It wouldn't have paid very well, either. There was a reason builders hired uneducated immigrants for those sorts of tasks.

We know he spent years – one long day at a time – carrying and setting bricks in that line of work. My aunts (John's granddaughters) still remember the scarring and discolorations that could be seen on his hands for decades after the fact. His fingers didn't seem to move as easily as they should have, and there must have been a great deal of pain in his later years. Still, he never complained about it or looked back on that part of his life with regret. He simply saw it as the first step toward a bigger destiny.

The other detail we have, from the stories he told later in life, is that my great-grandfather used to leave early for his job every morning. He rented a room that was several blocks from the construction site where he worked from day to day. Rather than talk to friends or gawk at the sights on the way to his job, like so many others did, he would scour the ground searching for loose change.

To hear Great-Grandfather John tell it, he got so adept at this that he would *almost always* be able to find a nickel somewhere on the way to work. That probably doesn't sound like a lot, and in truth it wasn't much even then. Over the course of a week, though, he could use those extra nickels to buy a meal, get shoes that fit, or even save a dollar here and there.

Many of the immigrants in that era would have been happy for a warm place to sleep and a weekly wage that allowed them to buy a few beers after work. My great-grandfather certainly was appreciative of what came to him, but he was also methodical about keeping extra money aside for his future plans.

All of that came a bit later, though. It's my belief that working as a bricklayer taught John all about foundations. In the literal sense, he saw that the right base could help you create an extraordinary building that could last for ages. And on a more metaphorical level, he learned that hard work and consistent effort were foundations on which you could build a successful career or business. Both of those lessons paid off in a big way over time.

John in his younger years.

Life isn't fair. It never has been, and probably never will be. All of us should be aware of the struggles that others are facing and do our part to make sure that we are building a world with plenty of opportunities for future generations. The one thing I've learned from hearing about my great-grandfather's childhood, however, is that unfairness isn't an excuse to give up. It certainly wasn't fair that he had to be broke and alone halfway across the world from his loved ones. But instead of complaining, he just made it work.

I wonder how much more we could all accomplish if we simply followed his example.

3

THE NEXT OPPORTUNITY

If my great-grandfather John had simply arrived at Ellis Island with nothing and worked his way through life as a bricklayer, that would have been enough to impress me. To suffer through those kinds of long days and difficult conditions says something about anyone's character.

Even though I don't know all the details of his life at that point, however, there is something I can be sure of: he was always looking ahead. My great-grandfather kept his eyes on the horizon, always knowing that his darkest days would lead to a new opportunity around the corner. Even when he developed frostbite in his fingers as a young man, he just kept working ahead.

The opportunity that eventually arrived wasn't an obvious one. He didn't win the lottery or find a wealthy benefactor. He simply saved what little amounts of money he could and paid attention to what was happening all around him.

In April of 1908 a fire broke out at the Boston Blacking Company on West Third Street in Chelsea, Massachusetts. Although firefighters arrived quickly, the heat spread at a faster rate than could be contained. In fact, the flames began to jump from one building to another until large parts of the city were enveloped.

Over the course of that day the Great Chelsea Fire consumed huge chunks of Boston. Nineteen people were killed. Entire blocks and neighborhoods were burned to the ground overnight. An estimated 1,500 buildings were destroyed, and more than 12,000 people found themselves without any place to live.

Chelsea Square after the great fire of 1908.

This was undoubtedly an enormous tragedy for the city, and even the country. Many would have been left with a sense of fear and uncertainty. It might have felt to them as if all were lost.

When Great-Grandfather John heard about the fire, his reaction was different. He would have been sad to hear about so much loss and pain. However, he also knew from experience that anything that had been destroyed could be rebuilt. He understood the power of starting again with the right foundations.

In the weeks following the Great Chelsea Fire he made a decision that would alter the course of his life and so many others'. Rather than continuing on as a bricklayer in New York City, he would take his hard-earned savings and move to Boston. Not only could he take what he had learned and help the city rebuild, but he could also become his own boss in the process.

Capobianco Construction was founded in 1908. I suppose that in one sense you could say the business grew out of tragedy and need. That's undoubtedly true – John seemed to sense when change was in the air. More than that, though, I think it was just his natural capacity for hope that brought the vision to life.

Even when he was young and came to America with nothing, he didn't lose his sense of purpose and passion. As easy as it would have been to feel sorry for himself, or settle for what had been given to him, he wanted to see what might be possible with time and determination. Later in life my great-grandfather was known as an extremely generous and giving person. I can't imagine, though, what it would have taken for him to save the pennies and nickels needed to start his own business. There must have been times when he wanted to give himself some little gift or luxury. Instead, he would just think about the future.

In some ways, that might be the greatest gift Great-Grandfather John left for me, and for all of us. It's one thing to talk about seeing the bright side of life or make a social media post about looking forward. When it really comes down to it, though, many of us are more comfortable thinking about what's going wrong than we are in looking for opportunities to improve our lives... or the lives of others.

My relatives used to tell a story about how, during the Great Depression, my great grandfather came across a man who was about to jump from a building. Apparently he'd lost all his money and couldn't see any hope for a brighter future. He didn't plead with the man to stay still. Instead, he just asked him whether he thought he'd find the money on the way down to the ground. In other words, had the man really arrived at a solution worth chasing? Or, would he definitely be making things worse?

The jumper did climb down, of course, after he realized that falling to his death wouldn't help anyone. It's a nice story, and one that kind of sums up what I know about my great grandfather's view of life.

Not a single person who knew John believes he was driven by money. That was just a byproduct of his hard work. So, when his neighbors to the north saw their homes and businesses disappear, it was only natural that his first instinct would have been to help out. He set off for a fresh start, once again, and never looked back.

Of course, it's easier to make those kinds of decisions when you're only risking your own future. John didn't have a family or employees to worry about when he arrived in Boston. That was going to change quickly enough.

4
A GROWING BUSINESS

A business finance consultant would probably have described John's Boston venture as "undercapitalized." In other words, he didn't have enough money. Neither did he have existing contacts in the city, or even experience running a business. He simply had a few dollars to get started and an absolute determination in his own ability to work his way to the top.

That's not much, but what else would you need if you had already survived life on your own in 19th-century New York City as a 12-year-old boy?

My point is that things would have been difficult, but my great-grandfather wasn't deterred. He knew how tough life could be, but also that the hard times never stayed forever. He simply kept doing what he did best and moved forward.

Great-Grandfather John would have walked through entire neighborhoods and districts that had been destroyed by fire, introducing himself to landlords, shopkeepers, and families needing to rebuild. After explaining that he had several years of experience working as a bricklayer, he would have told each one that he could help them start again with a better space than before. All he needed was a chance to prove himself.

I can't ever claim to fully appreciate most of the challenges my great-grandfather faced in his life. But as the founder of the digital agency named *GoingClear* in Boston, Massachusetts, this is one aspect of his life I can certainly relate to. No one who is starting their own company *ever* has the time, money, or knowledge they need. Resources are just too tight. It takes something incredibly brave – or maybe just optimistic – to put yourself out there and hope for the best.

Of course, things would have been even tougher in his day. Not only was his work much more physically demanding than mine, but employees and materials were all in short supply. The people who needed his help the most had just lost everything in tragic fashion. Not many of them had money to spend. And at the same time he wasn't the only one who recognized the new opportunity that existed in the construction business. There would have been larger firms flowing in from every part of the country.

Somehow John made it all work anyway. I have to imagine there was a bit of luck involved, but more than anything I think he simply refused to quit. He would have introduced himself to dozens or hundreds of people every day. We know he worked long hours guiding teams and supervising every aspect of the projects he accepted.

Success didn't come quickly. It was a constant battle to gather the materials he needed, get jobs finished on time, and meet payroll demands. There were difficult customers, new building codes, and ever-shrinking budgets. Competitors kept coming, including many that tried to undercut honest firms with scams or shoddy work.

Capobianco Construction's business postcard, promoting their offices at 44 School Street in Boston, Mass.

Still, as the months and years passed, Capobianco Construction kept moving forward. My great-grandfather developed a reputation for two things. The first was an attention to detail. No matter how busy his business became, or what kinds of challenges were thrown at him, he refused to cut corners. Maybe that's why so many of his buildings still grace the streets of Boston today.

The second thing Great-Grandfather John became known for was a commitment to honesty and integrity. His workers were paid what they were owed, even if it meant he had to go without for himself. He never asked anyone who worked for or with him to do something that was unethical. Neither would he request they do anything he wouldn't be willing to do himself. In an industry where employers treated customers and employees like enemies, he saw only friends and partners.

Within a few years, my great-grandfather had built a business that provided him with a comfortable middle-class life. One can imagine that a lot of immigrants would have been satisfied with that, particularly if they had traveled the same long road to reach that point. But John wanted to see if he could do even bigger things. Having come so far, he wondered whether he could turn his construction firm into the type that could bid for major projects.

Given his single-minded sense of determination, I think it would have been natural for him to start looking for ways to expand his business and bid on even bigger jobs. And he probably would have done exactly that, had it not been for the fact that something else caught his attention first.

First place award for a construction project in 1934.

5

ITALIA ROSE

In the decade following the Great Chelsea Fire, my great-grandfather felt like a blessed man. After starting with nothing he had learned a trade, built a business, and found the sort of opportunity that wouldn't have been available to him in the small Italian village where he grew up. He had his faith, his health, and enough money to take care of life's necessities.

The only thing missing at that point was what he might have secretly wanted the most: *a family*.

It isn't known among his surviving relatives whether John was looking to find a partner or if he was simply focused on his work when fate intervened. What they all agree on from the stories he told, however, is what came next.

One day John made his way into a family-owned market at the end of a busy East Boston street. The shop had fruit, flour, and other household items, but it was the young woman stocking the shelves who caught his eye. A quick conversation led him to understand that the shy and beautiful girl was part of the family that owned the store.

Her name was Italia Rose, owing to the fact that her family also originated from Italy. Unlike John, though, Italia had lived her whole life in America. She also happened to be a decade younger than he was. Neither of these facts bothered him. Those kinds of age differences between romantic partners were very common in his day, and there wasn't a huge difference between an Italian immigrant and someone who was the first child of Italian immigrants.

Besides, what my great-grandfather really cared about was the fact that he couldn't take his eyes off of the young woman he had met. Even though they only had a brief conversation, he told Italia that he meant to meet her parents and ask for her hand in marriage. And he did exactly that. The two were married just months later, in 1917.

> Mr. and Mrs. Giannario Casaletto
> request the honor of your presence
> at the marriage of their daughter
> Italia R.
> to
> Mr. John Capobianco
> on the evening of Monday, the eleventh of June
> one thousand nine hundred and seventeen
> at five o'clock
> at Walcott Hall, 32 Central Square
> East Boston, Massachusetts.

John and Italia's wedding invitation.

Viewed from a modern perspective it may seem as if they rushed into a relationship, but I don't think that at all. Obviously, ideas about courtship and dating were different then. Many people – and especially Italian immigrants – were family-focused, leading to a greater emphasis on marriage. What would seem reckless to us today probably felt normal to my great-grandmother's family.

More than that, I think there were two other issues that moved John to action. When he first met his wife he knew right away that she was the one. And, if life had taught him anything it was that you couldn't sit back or hesitate when the right decision was in front of you. You just had to act and trust in your own instincts. I think it would have killed him to know that his lifelong partner had gotten away when he was sure what he wanted and could see she felt the same way.

I also think my great-grandfather recognized immediately that the two had just the right mix of personalities. They complemented each other perfectly. John was outgoing, optimistic, and larger-than-life. He could bring a sense of energy and humor to any room where he walked in. Italia was more shy and reserved. She was warm, and could enjoy a good laugh, but didn't have her husband's gregarious nature.

There was something about the pair of them together that brought out the best in each. With his wife, Great-Grandfather John's warm and generous instincts were magnified. When John was in the room, Italia could be more relaxed and let her guard down. They found it easy to love one another and forge a friendship and partnership that endured to the ends of their lives.

Italia Rose Capobianco.

To me, the couple set an example that all of us could stand to follow. Never settle for anyone less than your perfect other half. But when you find them, don't be afraid to take the leap and love them as much as you can with your entire being.

It's amazing to me to think that a brief interaction in a market led to a happy marriage that lasted for decades. By all accounts John and Italia loved each other and the life they built together. In fact, it wasn't long after their wedding that the family started to grow.

John and Italia in their later years.

6
A FAMILY MAN

I sometimes think my great-grandfather was a man who arrived before his time. Don't get me wrong, he was certainly a success in his own era. It's just that I think he was ahead of his contemporaries when it came to understanding the meaning of success.

In today's world, sustainability, work-life balance, and social impact are buzzwords. But in his day most business owners sought to make as much as they could, as fast as they could, without worrying too much about the consequences. That's why it's so amazing that John's story is of a man who was driven to provide the best life he possibly could for his family and friends... not to squeeze out an extra nickel at any cost.

He and his new wife settled into family life very quickly. They were married in 1917 and their first daughter, Margaret (my grandmother, my mom's mom), was born the next year[1]. They had three more daughters, with Angelina, Josephine, and Evelyn all arriving in the next seven years. They also had a fifth daughter who didn't survive childbirth. That would have been a crushing blow to the young couple, but one that wasn't so unusual at that point in history.

While there are some things we have to piece together about John's life based on photos, paperwork, and intuition, one crystal-clear fact is that he lived for his family. Everything he did revolved around his wife, his daughters, and then eventually his grandkids – Barbara, Henry "Buddy," Joan, John, Marguerite (my mother), Judy, Janet, and Angela.

Work was important, and he put a lot of effort into it. But when it came to finding what mattered for him, my great-grandfather always put his loved ones first.

This was apparent even in the early days of his marriage. Although construction was (and is) a difficult business that required long hours, he would always find a way to make it home for dinner. Sundays were for mass, and then taking everyone for a drive. John loved the beach, and swimming, and would pile everyone into the car for a weekend trip to the shore whenever possible.

Even when those sorts of adventures weren't possible, he still found ways to spend time with his daughters. It could be a long day at the office, a weekend trip to a job site, or just a few hours spent looking through blueprints. If there was a way to make it work, he would have one or more of his offspring next to him. All of John's surviving grandkids have stories about skipping school or missing an appointment because they got caught up in an adventure with Grandfather. He knew the value of face-to-face time with the people who were most important to him.

This also extended to others in the neighborhood. Despite the fact that he had so many demands on his schedule, Great-Grandpa John was known as someone you could come to for a favor or rely upon in an emergency. He was always active, but never too busy to help or listen.

Although a lot of that could be attributed to his big heart, it's probably also true that my great-grandfather just didn't like to sit still. He believed we were being our best selves when we were moving forward. Or, if there wasn't a goal or task to be finished then you could explore your faith.

My aunt Judy, one of John's granddaughters, tells a story I've always enjoyed. One Saturday morning, when she was a teenager, she made the mistake of mentioning to my great-grandfather that she was bored. He actually seemed shocked at the suggestion. How could anyone not be interested in the world with so much going on around them at all times? To help her snap out of it he took her to church for the day. I'm not sure that solved her problem, but it did keep her from ever using "the B word" out loud in his presence again.

To say that Great-Grandfather John was a family man who loved his wife, his daughters, and his grandchildren might not make for compelling reading. It's certainly not as exciting as his journey to New York, or the life-and-death adventure I'll describe in a coming chapter. However, I think it really gets to the essence of who he was, why he was so successful, and what made him happy. It's probably also the reason so many people remember him as being a wonderful man five decades after he left the earth.

Isn't that the sort of life we should all be trying to live? And aren't those the memories we want to leave behind?

7
DINNERTIME

In interviewing different members of the family about my great-grandfather, there was one aspect of his life as a family man that came up again and again. Each of them spoke about his dinnertime ritual.

In 1920, just a few years after his marriage to Italia Rose, John decided he needed a bigger house for his growing family. His vision became the multistoried property that still sits at 129 Chiswick Road in Brighton, on the outskirts of Boston.

At first, John lived on the ground floor with his wife and daughters. The other floors were divided into apartments that were rented to tenants. Over time, as his daughters married, husbands and grandchildren filled many of those additional spaces.

The building John built on Chiswick Road in Brighton, Mass. where his family lived.

The entire place was built as an oasis for the Capobianco clan. There were two sculpted lions guarding the front door, and the first floor opened into an atrium. There was a sunroom, marble countertops, and a huge back garden with grapevines and orange trees brought over from Italy. In the back were habitats for canaries and parakeets, adding to the fairytale feeling throughout the property.

As wonderful as these extra touches were, though, the kitchen was the clear centerpiece of the home. Not only were there large countertops and cooking areas, but also a breakfast nook that could seat 15. There was also a long horseshoe-shaped table, specially designed at John's request, that made it possible for the entire family to sit together for dinner.

Many of John's beloved grandchildren around the table. Pictured from left to right: Marie, Angie, Barbara, Johnny, Great Grandfather John, Buddy, Marguerite, Vee, Bud, Henry, Great Grandmother Italia, and Margaret.

That was the part of the day the John lived for. The rest of the family loved it, too. At 6 o'clock sharp it was time to eat and share. It didn't matter what you were doing; you *had* to be there. There was nothing to do with work, school, or any other distraction that could keep you away. Dinner was just the time when family got together, and he wouldn't accept any excuses.

Being at dinner on time was mandatory. The only other rule was that there couldn't be any arguing at the table. Everyone could talk, and long hours were spent laughing together. The discussion was lively but light. John's favorite way to break the ice would be to tease his wife. He liked to fold up a napkin and tickle her ear when she wasn't looking. She would express mock anger and everyone would be in on the joke.

During this time of day the kids might talk among themselves, siblings and cousins, catching up on school or hobbies. Or, the older family members might share experiences. Often the entire family was involved. Perhaps something from the news, or a recent sermon might be discussed. John could share an anecdote from a work site, or talk about something interesting he had read in the paper. It didn't matter. There was never a set topic or agenda. Instead, it was a chance for everyone to be present and connected.

John and Italia having fun with their grandchildren.

The meals themselves were glorious. The first course would usually be a salad, which was little more than lettuce with some bread and olive oil on the side. It was just something light before the real show began. My great-grandmother was a wonderful cook and would prepare dishes like homemade lasagna, chicken cutlets, and large ribeye steaks. Those left everyone feeling full and satisfied. Afterward there would be desserts made from fresh apples and pears (also grown in the backyard). Her pies, or poached treats drizzled with caramel, are still remembered with great joy.

As you can imagine, there was never any hurry to finish a meal. Between the talking, eating, and laughing, dinner might stretch on for hours. When everyone had finished, by 10 or 11 at night, John would finish the day with a cup of coffee. If it had been a good day or evening he might stir in a small spoonful of scotch and enjoy a sense of peace and satisfaction. I can imagine that with a full stomach and the house filled with loved ones, he was at his happiest, most contented self.

John, 5th from the right, at a celebration after he broke new ground on a construction project.

I can't remember these dinners. Unfortunately they ended years before I was born. What always strikes me when I hear about them, though – besides the wonderful food that I would have loved to have tried – is the way my older relatives talk about them so warmly. Even with such a large family, and everyone spending time together every night, no one was ever uncomfortable or left out.

From right to left: my grandfather Alphonse Scott, Great-Grandfather John, Mae Gallo, Governor John Volpe, and colleagues.

My aunts, who were John's granddaughters, reminisce about those dinners as being some of the best moments in their lives. It wasn't the big house that made them special, or even the gourmet cooking. Those things helped, but what they really remember (and miss most) was the way their grandfather made them feel. When you were having dinner with him, you knew there was nowhere else in the entire world he wanted to be. It made him happy just to share that time with you.

That's a lesson I try to bring to my own home. Are you doing all you can to spend meaningful time with the people who mean the most to you?

A family picture.

8

BECOMING A LEGEND

It may be that some people thrive in an environment of change and chaos, but I believe my great-grandfather was someone who valued stability. With peace and a loving family at home, it was easier for him to focus on bigger goals and tasks at work. And so, as his family grew so did his sense of ambition. With his loving wife and daughters at his side, John entered what I have to imagine was the best period of his life.

Professionally, he was taking on bigger and more complex projects. He didn't work the way some construction entrepreneurs did. Rather than focusing on a certain type of building, he simply looked for projects that excited him or could make a difference in the community.

A picture taken at a Capobianco Construction job site.

Within my family there is an old portfolio book showing completed Capobianco Construction projects all around Boston, Waltham, and the North Shore. There are photos of hospitals, schools, office buildings, and apartments. There is a house he built for one of his daughters on Cape Cod, and of course the old family home on Chiswick Road. To look at them doesn't just give you a sense of history. You also get a feeling of pride.

Many of these buildings still sit throughout the greater Boston area. There are also other reminders of his hard work. Recently, I had the chance to take an autumn drive through the Kancamagus Highway in northern New Hampshire – known as one of the most scenic in New England. When it was being built in the 1930s the planners and engineers needed to find someone they could trust to do a difficult job. They turned to my great-grandfather for help blasting through the mountainous rock, knowing he would handle the job safely and for a fair price.

However, the most notable of the Capobianco Construction buildings (at least to me) is the St. Anthony's Church in Revere, Massachusetts . It's the place where I was married to my wife, Lauren, and where our daughter Mary was baptized.

St. Anthony's Church in Revere, Mass. around the time it was completed in the 1920s.

St. Anthony's Church in Revere, Mass. in 2022.

It's incredible to think of all that my great-grandfather helped build. What's even more amazing is that he did it after starting from nothing, and while treating his customers and coworkers with respect. My mother and aunts would remind me how John used to say that "all you have is your name and your word." That small piece of advice holds up just as well today as it did a hundred years ago.

A picture of John Capobionco in one of his favorite hats.

Unfortunately, not everyone is quite so honest and my great-grandfather could be trusting to a fault. Despite his difficult early years, he never became skeptical or hardened. He always looked for the best in others.

At some point in the 1930s John was introduced to a pair of men who claimed they were interested in partnering with him on a construction project in New York City. None of his surviving relatives remember the exact details, but it was a big job with the potential to leave a lasting mark on the city where everything had started for him. Presumably, he would have been excited to return to the Big Apple and provide jobs and opportunities for others, like himself, who were trying to get a start in construction.

The terms of the deal were set and the men invited my great-grandfather to travel south with them by train. Like a lot of people who had lived through the Great Depression, John wasn't especially trustful of banks. He decided to bring his portion of the investment – $1 million in cash – along with him in a briefcase.

When the train got near the city, the two men made an excuse to get off one stop early. From there, they led my great-grandfather to a set of empty tracks. Once they had reached a quiet area, the first man pulled a gun from his jacket and pointed it in John's direction. The two thieves had a quick and quiet conversation with one another. It ended when the second said to his accomplice: "Kill him."

The unarmed man walked away, leaving the other two in a deadly silence. My great-grandfather didn't panic or make threats. He simply said to his would-be killer: "I have small kids and a wife who need me."

Maybe something changed in that man's heart when he realized my great-grandfather had a growing family at home. Perhaps he just didn't have the nerve to follow through with his intended plan. Whatever the reason, he offered John a simple take-it-or-leave-it offer: "Keep walking down these tracks. Don't look back. And never return to this place or contact us again."

John nodded his head and started walking. He never did look back, in that moment or ever after. He didn't even try to recover his money; he was happy enough to just have another chance at life. In fact, he remembered that criminal who spared him almost like a friend. He always remembered the man had been Jewish and he developed an affinity for those who followed that faith.

I can't imagine how big your heart would have to be to get over something like that without being bitter or disillusioned. But I guess it was all part of becoming a legend.

9

THE FULLNESS OF LIFE

There are a lot of different ways you can handle success and setbacks. In the same way that my great-grandfather never let money or prestige go to his head, neither would he let the disappointment of being robbed for a million dollars change him. He just told his family, when he finally shared the story, that it was only his luck and success that had made him a target in the first place.

If anything, I think the experience gave him a new appreciation for his life and his loved ones.

In our time, the internet is full of posts about the healing power of positive energy, even as that optimism seems conspicuously absent from so many people's lives. And yet, for Great-Grandfather John it wasn't just talk. He always emphasized the need to forgive others, and to be loyal to your word. But mostly, he simply did everything he could to squeeze the most out of his time on Earth.

His business continued to grow and thrive, of course, and managing projects took a great deal of time. Besides the ledgers and blueprints that would keep anyone in his position busy, he also made a point of visiting job sites frequently. Sometimes he would even take a break from being the boss to lay bricks with his men. They would always mention how much they appreciated the fact that he was willing to get his own hands dirty. But I don't think these bits of manual labor were only about leadership. I think my great-grandfather liked to remind himself of where he came from as frequently as possible.

Besides, he was certainly up to the physical effort. While he could easily have grown fat and satisfied (literally and figuratively) from the profits of his company, he always strove to remain lean and agile. Aside from his hands-on construction work, John walked several blocks to and from mass almost every day. If possible, he would recruit other members of the family to bring with him. It was a way to stay fit, deepen those bonds, and keep his faith intact all at the same time.

When he wasn't at work or at church, Great-Grandfather John was one of those people who had the almost magic ability to seem like they were everywhere at once. You might find him picking homegrown oranges from his yard. Or he could be helping a neighbor with a home repair project. He also liked to take a stroll around the neighborhood with one of his closest friends, a local rabbi.

As his daughters married and the family grew, there were weddings, births, and too many celebrations to count. From time to time he would travel back to Italy, catching up with his brother or visiting the village where he was born. The family legend is that the couple almost always traveled via cruise because Italia held onto a lifelong fear of flying.

Although America was changing quickly, Sturno remained largely as it had in his childhood memories. I can't even imagine the sense of pride he must have felt returning to those old town squares he had walked as a child and seeing them once again as a man who had fulfilled his destiny.

John and Italia on a cruise ship.

That destiny made him a man with several different parts to his identity. Some might have struggled with different backgrounds pulling them in different directions, but he seemed to be at ease with his own mind and values. He was Italian born, for example, but also an American success story. He was able to separate the past from the present. In fact, when World War II broke out he was one of the most prominent Italian Americans to call on Mussolini to lay down arms while speaking on WBZ radio in Boston.

Prelate's Brother Urges Italy to Quit

Continuing the highly effectvie shortwave broadcasts to Italy that have taken their part in history in the downfall of Benito Mussolini as head of the Italian government, American patriots of Italian descent today beseeched their kinfolk to accept the United Nations' peace terms.

Prominent among the messages beamed overseas today was one from John Capobianco, leading Boston contractor and one of the most highly respected Italian-American citizens in this section of the nation.

A native of Sturno, in the Province of Avellino, and well known in Italy as the brother of Msgr. Angelo Capobianco, noted Catholic prelate, Capobianco told of the friendly and sympathetic welcome he received when he came to America as a boy of 13. Emphasizing that Americans are a peace-loving people, he said:

"I urge you, as one who has made many trips back to the homeland since first settling in America, to make every effort to bring about an early peace. Pray for it! Work for it! Lay down your arms!

LAY DOWN ARMS

"Do not make beautiful Italy a battleground. Accept the honorable peace which President Roosevelt has offered you."

Capobianco's appeal was one of scores arranged in New England by the Daily Record-American-Sunday Advertiser.

Simultaneously, in 14 key cities throughout the nation, affiliated Hearst newspapers are having similarly compelling messages recorded for broadcasts to Italy over high-powered ultra high frequency radio transmitters.

FOUR TIMES DAILY

Four times daily these broad- are sent to Africa and London for rebroadcast by the Algiers radio and the British Broadcasting Corporation.

Transcriptions are being made daily in Boston at radio station WBZ, which is co-operating with the Daily Record-American-Sunday Advertiser and the Office of War Information in the nationwide program to speed the war's end.

The speakers and recordings are being arranged by a Boston committee of Americans of Italian parentage headed by Stephen D. Bacigalupo, senior legal assistant of the Massachusetts appellate tax board.

Newspaper clipping from 1943 reporting on John's interview with WBZ radio in Boston.

The years stretched on, but Great-Grandfather John never lost his sense of wonder about life and the world around him. Every day was a new adventure, and also a chance to pass on the love and wisdom that lived in his heart. Wherever he was, and whomever he was with, he shared the values of friendship and kindness. He wanted everyone he met to know that they could find the same sense of material success and inner peace he had, if only they were willing to work hard and see the good in others.

It's ironic that my great-grandfather entered this portion of his life when he did. His big adventures were winding down just as photographs and printed records were improving. In other words, his life was becoming more comfortable right at the moment when it would have been easier than ever to tell the most vivid parts of his story. Who knows how much better, and more detailed, this book could have been if he had left more visual evidence behind?

Still, I don't think he would have minded. One of the many lessons I've drawn from his life is that you have to enjoy every day, and every moment, for what it is. There would have been so many triumphs and ribbon cuttings, not to mention occasions where he could rub elbows with important people like his very good friend Massachusetts Governor John Volpe, who served multiple terms in the early 1960's.

There are entire scrapbooks littered with photos like that one. I've seen one where he's sitting next to JFK and other leaders of the time. In another story that was passed down he spent an afternoon with the boxing great, Rocky Marciano. Rocky had come to visit John at his home in Cape Cod, bringing his wife, daughter, and new puppy along for the ride. I'm not sure how they met, but I'm told they spent the afternoon eating and laughing.

John with JFK, 35th President of the United States.

I don't doubt that Great-Grandfather John enjoyed those occasions, but I suspect they didn't live up to the family dinners he *really* looked forward to.

We might not know everything we would like to about John's life, especially during his early years. But we know he worked his way to the top and managed something that very few in that position ever can – to be loved, happy, and content.

Of course, nothing lasts forever. Even the most noteworthy lives come to an end. But even as my great-grandfather left this world, he had another lesson to bestow.

10

MY GREAT-GRANDFATHER'S LEGACY

John Capobianco passed away on April 30, 1969, due to sudden heart failure. He lived to be nearly 81 years old, still mentally and physically active right until the day he left us. None of his remaining grandchildren can remember him ever being sick for a day in his life before that point.

Great-Grandfather John was buried in Brighton, Massachusetts, next to a small church just outside of Boston where many prominent families from the area were laid to rest. True to form, he didn't just plan ahead for his own passing – he bought nearly two dozen plots so that the whole family could stay together for eternity. Even today I can see how thoughtful that was. His last wish was to have his family next to him around a heavenly dinner table as each one passed on, so having them together was important to him.

> CAPOBIANCO—John, in Brighton, Apr. 30, 1969. Beloved husband of Rose (Casaletto) Capobianco and beloved father of Mrs. Alphonse (Margaret) Scott, Mrs. Henry (Angela) Maffeo and Mrs. Evelyn Schuster, all of Brighton. Also survived by 8 grandchildren.

His passing was a huge blow to those who knew and loved him. Friends and associates from all around the country attended the funeral. To this day, surviving family members say he was the kindest, most loving, and most influential person they have ever known. As great as his ambition and business acumen were, no one talks about that. Instead, they just mention the talent he had for making every person feel special and valued.

The loss wasn't just felt within his family, of course. The company that bore his name would also need to be managed without its founder and guiding force. Although he had been very intentional when it came to having his loved ones close in the next life, his vision for what would happen to the Capobianco Construction Company was a bit murkier. It was probably the case that he simply wasn't as concerned. He knew his wife and children were well provided for. What else could there be to worry about? Or, maybe he just assumed (as most of us do) that he had more time remaining.

In any case, my great-grandmother suddenly found herself at the head of a multimillion-dollar corporation. She was a bright and competent woman but hadn't taken an active role in the business before that point. It's also fair to wonder whether her heart was truly in the endeavor. She was known to ask her children, after her husband had died, what it was she had left to live for.

Italia Rose outlived her husband by nine years, eventually succumbing to pancreatic cancer. Although she was greatly missed by her children, grandchildren, and even great-grandchildren by that point, it may have been a blessing. The grief and physical pain she had suffered through after John died would have been difficult to endure.

With both John and Italia gone, the family – and the family business with it – started to splinter. It may have been the case that either had grown too large and distant to hold together. The children and grandchildren stopped having dinner together. Relationships grew more strained. There were disagreements about keepsakes, inheritances, and responsibilities.

Different relatives tried their hands at managing the corporation; none of them found lasting success. After a few years new construction projects ceased and the focus shifted to managing properties and collecting rents. Still, the company struggled to sustain itself without John as its guiding force.

Eventually, executives were brought in from outside the family. Perhaps it was too late, or the Boston commercial real estate market was changing too quickly. Maybe my great-grandfather was just too important to the functioning of the business for it to survive without him. One way or another, the remaining properties were eventually sold and the funds were disbursed among the surviving heirs.

I suppose you could think of this as a kind of tragedy. Not only did a large and thriving business dissolve within a generation, but that process was accelerated by a lack of unity within the family. I may not have met my great-grandfather, but I know that was the opposite of what he would have wanted for his surviving loved ones and their descendants.

But on the other hand, his legacy was so much bigger than a corporation. There are still around a dozen key commercial buildings across Boston that he built. They have stood the test of time and still make the city I love a more beautiful place.

His impact is still felt in the family and community, too. The fortune he amassed might be gone, but the example he set for the rest of us remains. It's the spirit that inspired me to start my own business, to gather what I could learn about his life, and to publish this book. I like to think my great-grandfather would be proud of my work, and could see the parallels between his efforts and my own. He built wonderful physical structures across New England. My work is virtual, but the B2B websites I've created for my clients have done just as much for their companies. It's the same drive and mission, but in a different era.

That's because his most important lessons were timeless. When you have the right values and a sense of determination you can accomplish virtually anything. While I'm guessing Great-Grandfather John might be disappointed to know that his construction company is no longer functioning as a business, he would understand that it was never the profits or properties that mattered. Families and fortunes can be rebuilt. You just have to have the right foundations.

THANK YOU, JOHN

When I first began this project I wasn't sure what I was trying to accomplish. I knew it would be impossible to put together a biography about my great-grandfather, given the gaps we have in knowledge and documentation about his life. Too much time has passed, and too many people who knew him are gone. My own mom, Marguerite, passed away in August 2021 while I was writing. I would have loved for her to see the finished version, but I feel glad to know she had a chance to contribute directly to this book. I know my Aunt Judy, who was a huge help with a lot of these stories, will love this book.

Neither did I want this to be a simple recounting of stories or life and business lessons. Those are important, but there are plenty of books like that available. And besides, while I might draw some of my own conclusions from Great-Grandfather John's life, it didn't feel right to give his opinions for him after the fact.

As I began collecting stories and documents, however, I realized that what I *really* wanted was a way to thank the man who did so much for me and my family. In that way, this short book is my attempt to know him a bit better and pass on my gratitude for all that he achieved and left us with. It's my thank-you note to him half a century later.

While I never got to have dinner with my great-grandfather, he has always been a part of my life. My mother talked about him all the time. His pictures fill our home, and whenever we would pass a building he had constructed my mom would point it out. That was especially true of Saint Anthony's church of Revere, Massachusetts he built. He loved to take his grandkids there and even now I attend with my wife, Lauren, daughter Mary, and baby to be. We sit in the same seats he did on Sundays.

If John were here today I would take the chance to ask him about all the parts of his life I don't know about. I would want to know how he managed to get by as a 12-year-old living alone in New York City. I would let him tell me exactly what it was that led him to fall in love with my great-grandmother in the first moment they met. I would want to hear more about the thoughts that must have raced through his mind while he was being held at gunpoint.

More than any of that, though, I would just want to tell him "Thank you" and let him know that I am trying to live up to his example. He managed to leave a legacy filled with joy and inspiration. He reminded everyone he knew that real success was about family, being present, working smart, forward thinking, having the right team, and doing the right thing even when it was tough. He cared about attention to detail when it came to developing properties without making him too focused on work or the bottom line. I'll continue to serve forward and live a life worth celebrating as he did.

Thank you, Great-Grandfather!

APPENDIX: CAPOBIANCO CONSTRUCTION PHOTOS

St. John's Seminary, (Library Building) Brighton, Mass.

Regis College, Weston, Mass.

St. Andrew's Church, Forest Hills, Mass.

Greek Church, Boston, Mass.

St. Lazarus Church, East Boston, Mass.

Church of Our Lady
Waltham, Mass.

St. Benedict's School
Somerville, Mass.

Apartment Block, Brighton, Mass.

General Motors Truck Building, Brighton, Mass.

NOTES

6. A Family Man

1. My grandmother Margaret (John's daughter and my mom's mom) actually became one of the first female judges in Massachusetts, and one of the first Italian-Americans appointed to the judicial bench.

www.ingramcontent.com/pod-product-compliance
Lightning Source LLC
Chambersburg PA
CBHW020736020526
44118CB00033B/955